A JOHN DENVER CHRISTMAS

S0-ACE-049

ISBN 1-57560-131-1

Songs originally recorded by John Denver on the albums *Rocky Mountain Christmas* and *John Denver & The Muppets: A Christmas Together*.

Visit our website at www.cherrylane.com

A JOHN DENVER CHRISTMAS

AWAY IN A MANGER

Traditional

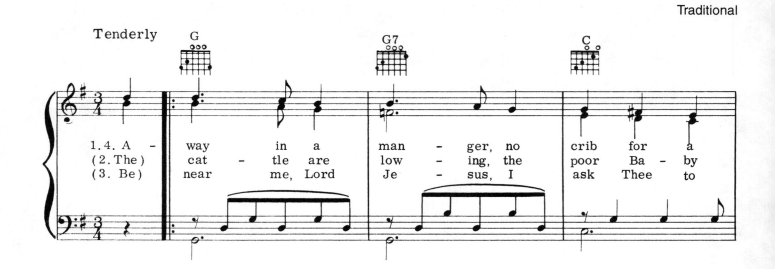

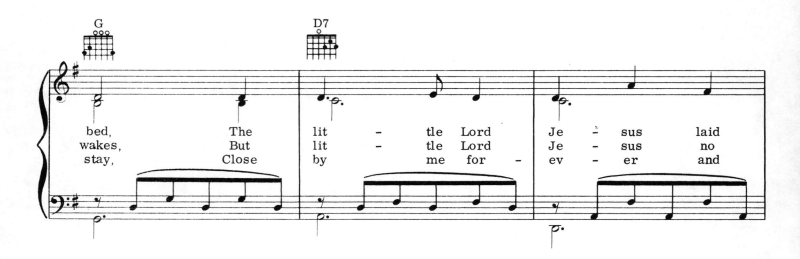

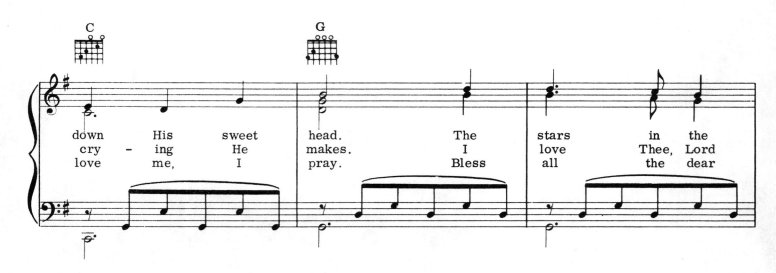

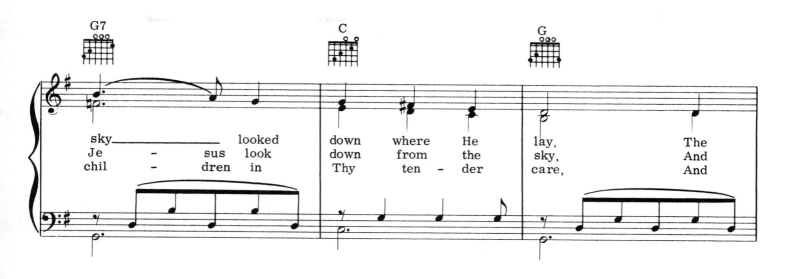

sky _____ looked down where He lay, The
Je - sus look down from the sky, And
chil - dren in Thy ten - der care, And

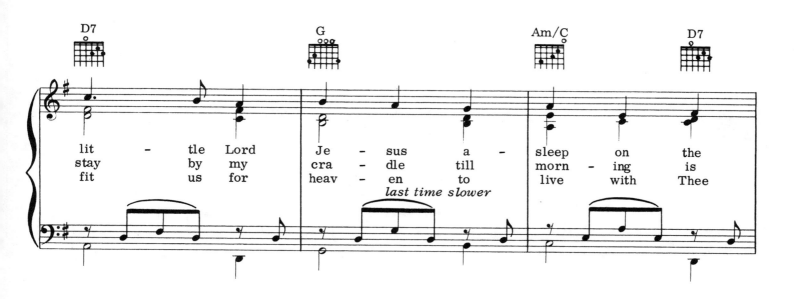

lit - tle Lord Je - sus a - sleep on the
stay by my cra - dle till morn - ing is
fit us for heav - en to live with Thee

last time slower

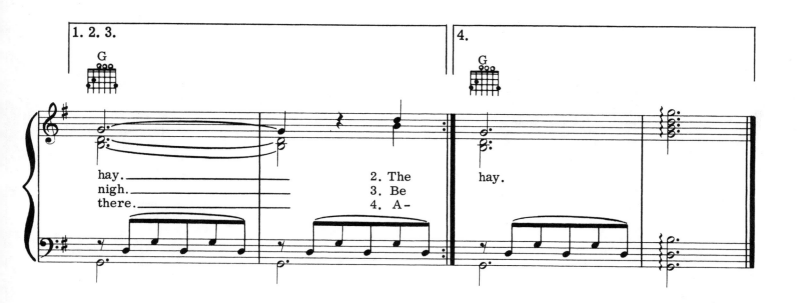

hay. _____
nigh. _____
there. _____

2. The
3. Be
4. A-

hay.

A BABY JUST LIKE YOU

Words and Music by John Denver
and Joe Henry

Oh, lit-tle an - gel, shin - ing light, you've set my soul to dream - ing. You've giv - en back my joy in life and filled me with new mean - ing.

It's just a wish, a dream I'm told, from

8

CAROL FOR A CHRISTMAS TREE

Music by Lee Holdridge

CHRISTMAS LIKE A LULLABY

Words and Music by
John Denver

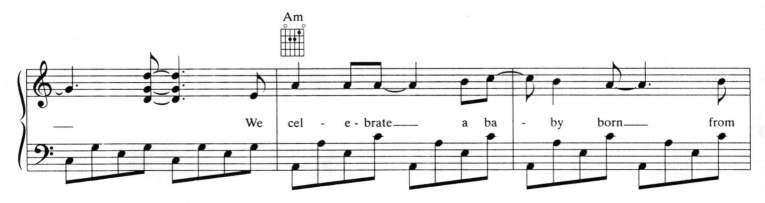

* Recorded a half step higher

nev - er seemed____ so   ver - y far____ a - way,____

back where night____ has   fall - en   and it's still____ Christ - mas   Eve.____

____   And   snow is in____ the   moun - tains   that   I

al - ways____ hate to   leave.____   But

here   I   am____   down   un - der   with a   brand - new____   fam - i - ly.____

on   this   morn - ing   peace____   on   earth   is   still   our____   fer - vent   prayer,

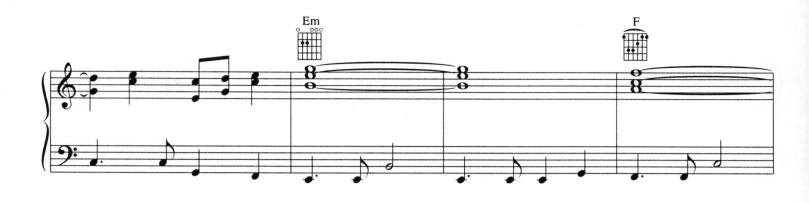

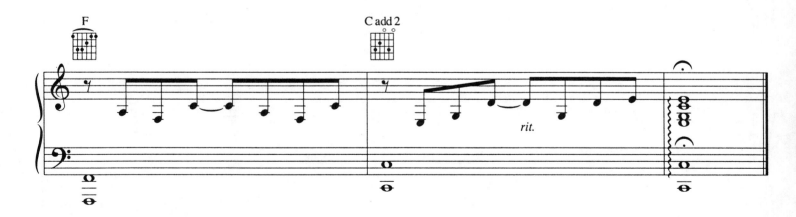

CHRISTMAS FOR COWBOYS

Words and Music by
Steve Weisberg

CHRISTMAS IS COMING

Traditional English Carol

The two chords used in this round are

(Round)

22

THE CHRISTMAS WISH

Words and Music by
Danny Allen Wheetman

1. I don't know if you be-lieve in Christ-mas
2. For I have held the prec-ious gift that love brings
3. For the truth that binds us all to-geth-er

E-ven though Or if you have pres-ents un-der-
I would like to say a sim-ple

Bb   C   Bb

neath   the   Christ - mas   tree, ____
star. ____
prayer; ____   But if   you   be -
        I   know   there
        That at   there   this

C   F   Am7   Bb /D   F/C

lieve   in   love ____
is   a   light, ____
spe - cial   time ____   that will   be
   I have felt   it
   you will have   more   than e - nough   For
   burn in - side,   And
   true   peace of mind   And

Bb   C7   F

To Coda

you   to come   and
I   have seen   it
love   to last   through   cel - e - brate ____ with
   shin - ing ____ from a -
       me.
       far.

1.   2.
C7   F7   Bb

Christ - mas is   the

25

out   the   com - ing   year.

THE CHRISTMAS SONG
(CHESTNUTS ROASTING ON AN OPEN FIRE)

Music and Lyric by Mel Torme
and Robert Wells

THE COVENTRY CAROL

Words by Robert Croo
Traditional English Melody

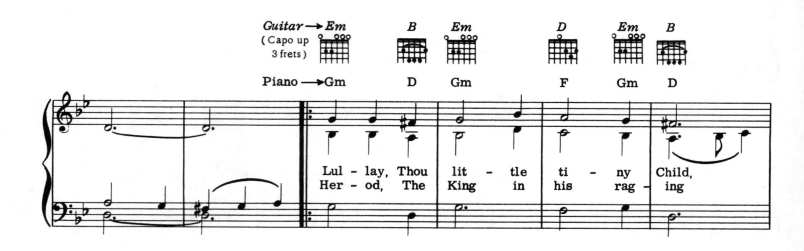

Lul - lay, Thou lit - tle ti - ny Child,
Her - od, The King in his rag - ing

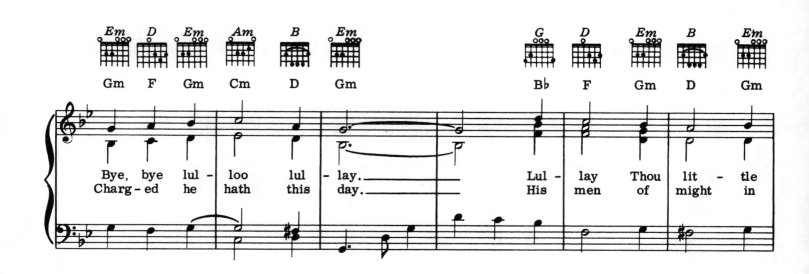

Bye, bye lul - loo lul - lay. _____
Charg - ed he hath this day. _____

Lul - lay Thou lit - tle
His men of might in

DECK THE HALLS

Traditional Welsh Carol

THE FIRST NOEL

17th Century English Carol

cold win-ter's night____ that was____ so deep. No-
ël,_____ No-ël, No-ël, No-
ël, Born is the King____ of
Is-ra-el. The____ Is-ra-el.

37

GO TELL IT ON THE MOUNTAIN

African-American Spiritual

GOD REST YE MERRY, GENTLEMEN

19th Century English Carol

Brightly

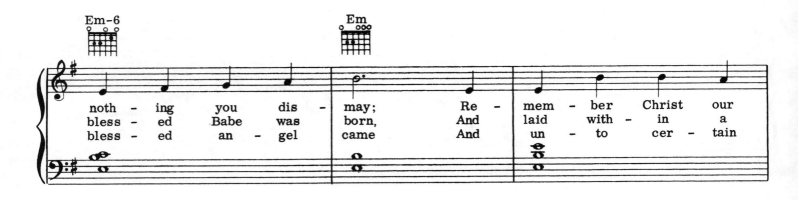

41

HARK! THE HERALD ANGELS SING

Words by Charles Wesley
Music by Felix Mendelssohn-Bartholdy

Firmly

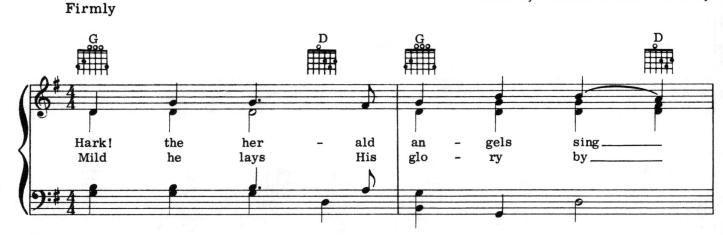

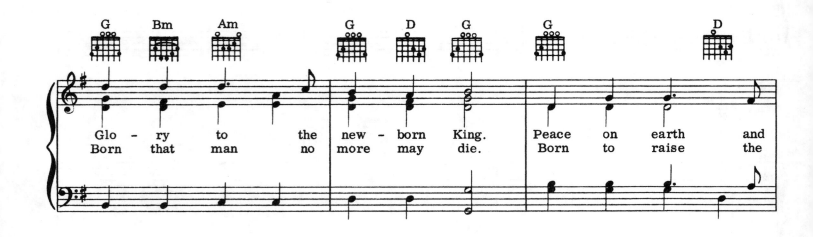

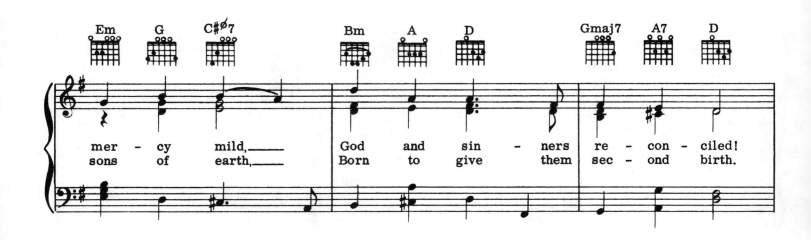

HERE WE COME A-CAROLING

Traditional

With spirit

Here we come a - car - ol - ing A -
We are not dai - ly beg - gars that
Bless the mas - ter of this house like -

mong the leaves so green; Here we come a -
beg from door to door, And We are neigh - bor's
wise the mis - tress too, all the lit - tle

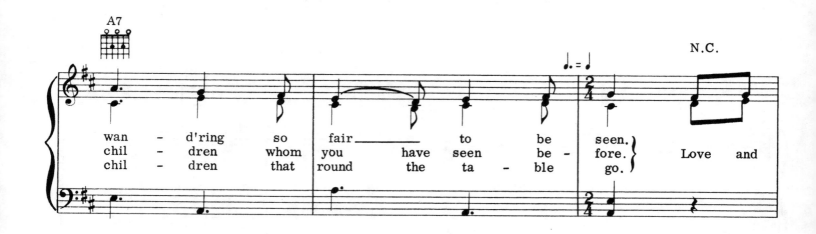

wan - d'ring so fair____ to be seen. Love and
chil - dren whom you have seen be - fore.
chil - dren that round the ta - ble go.

I SAW THREE SHIPS

Traditional English Carol

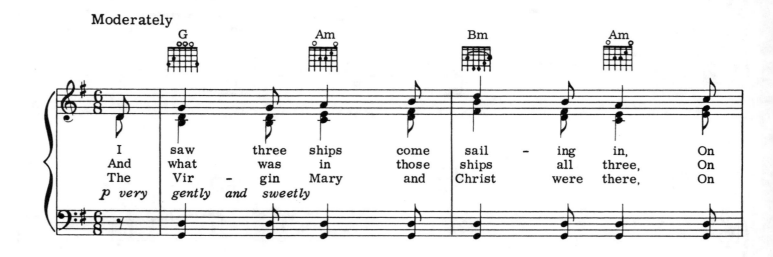

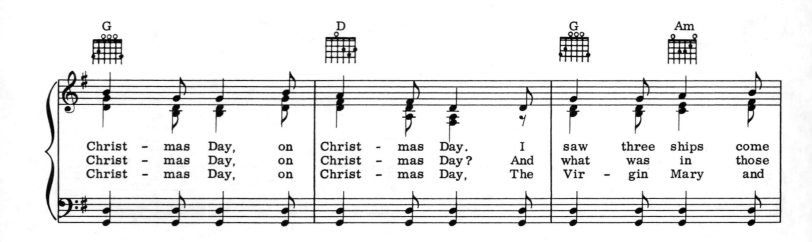

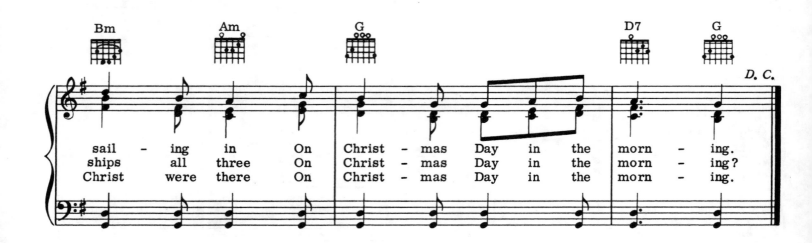

THE MARVELOUS TOY

Words and Music by
Tom Paxton

bright, and the mo- ment I___ laid eyes on it, it be- came my heart's de- light. It went "zip" when it moved, "bop" when it stopped, "whirr" when it stood still. I nev- er knew___ just what it was___ and I guess I nev- er will.

Chorus

1.2.3.

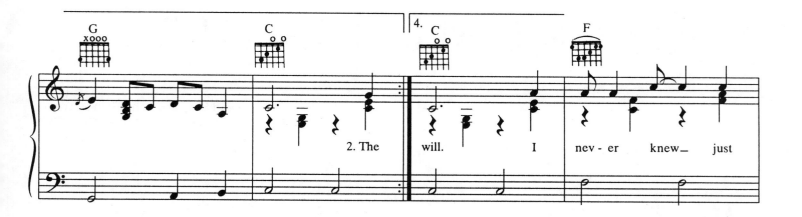

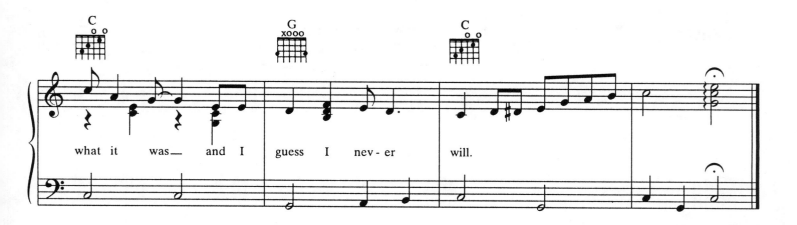

Additional Lyrics

2. The first time that I picked it up, I had a big surprise,
   For right on its bottom were two green buttons that looked like big green eyes.
   I first pushed one and then the other, and then I twisted its lid,
   And when I set it down again, this is what it did: *(To Chorus)*

3. It first marched left and then marched right and then marched under a chair,
   And when I looked where it had gone, it wasn't even there!
   I started to cry; my daddy laughed; he knew that I would find
   When I turned around my marvelous toy, chugging from behind. *(To Chorus)*

4. Well, the years have passed too quickly, it seems; I have my own little boy.
   And yesterday I gave to him my marvelous little toy.
   His eyes nearly popped right out of his head; he gave a squeal of glee.
   Neither one of us knows just what it is, but he loves it, just like me.

Final Chorus: It still goes "zip" when it moves, "bop" when it stops,
   "Whirr" when it stands still.
   I never knew just what it was,
   And I guess I never will.
   I never knew just what it was,
   And I guess I never will.

O COME, ALL YE FAITHFUL

Words and Music by John Francis Wade
Latin Words translated by Frederick Oakeley

Majestically

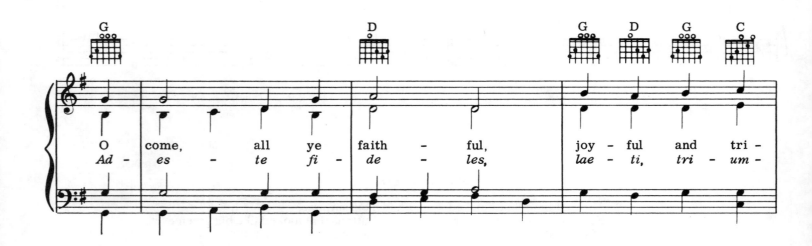

O come, all ye faith - ful, joy - ful and tri -
Ad - es - te fi - de - les, lae - ti, tri - um -

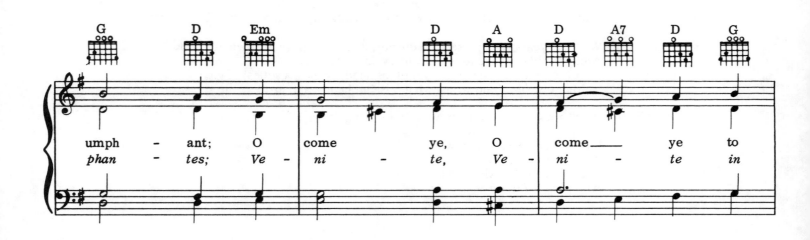

umph - ant; O come ye, O come___ ye to
phan - tes; Ve - ni - te, Ve - ni - te in

Beth - - le - hem.
Beth - - le - hem.

Come and be -
Na - tum vi -

hold Him born the King of an - gels: O
de - te, Re - gum an - ge - lo - rum: Ve -

come let us a - dore Him, O come, let us a - dore Him, O
ni - te ad - o - re - mus, Ve - ni - te ad - o - re - mus, Ve -

come let us a - dore Him,___ Christ_____ the Lord.
ni - te ad - o - re - mus___ Do - mi - num.

D.C.

O HOLY NIGHT

French Words by Placide Cappeau
English Words by D.S. Dwight
Music by Adolphe Adam

Moderately

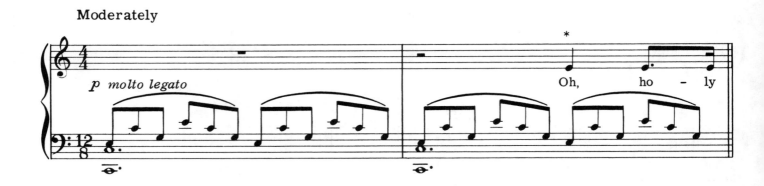

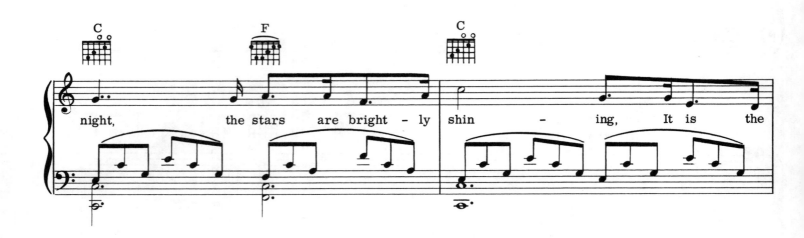

* *In presence of voice or melody instrument, piano should omit the melody.*

THE PEACE CAROL

Words and Music by
Bob Beers

57

PLEASE DADDY
(DON'T GET DRUNK THIS CHRISTMAS)

Words and Music by Bill Danoff
and Taffy Danoff

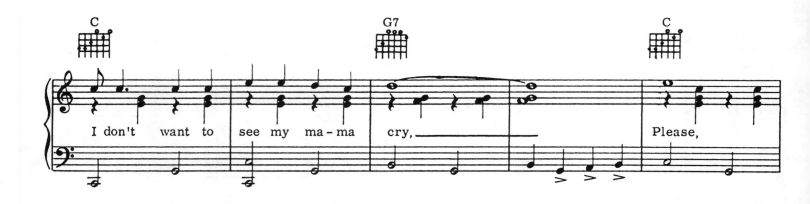

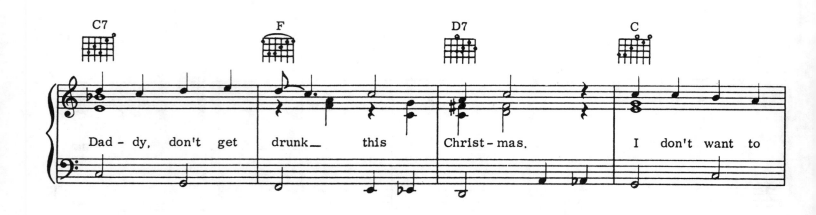

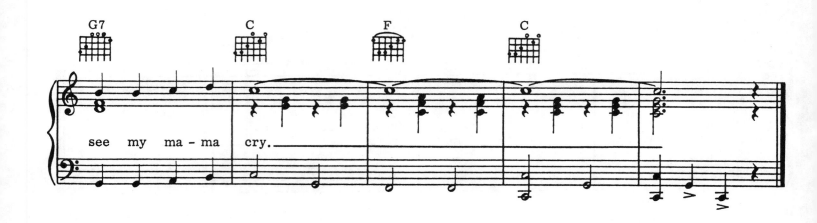

RUDOLPH THE
RED-NOSED REINDEER

Music and Lyrics by
Johnny Marks

SILENT NIGHT, HOLY NIGHT

Words by Joseph Mohr
Music by Franz Grüber

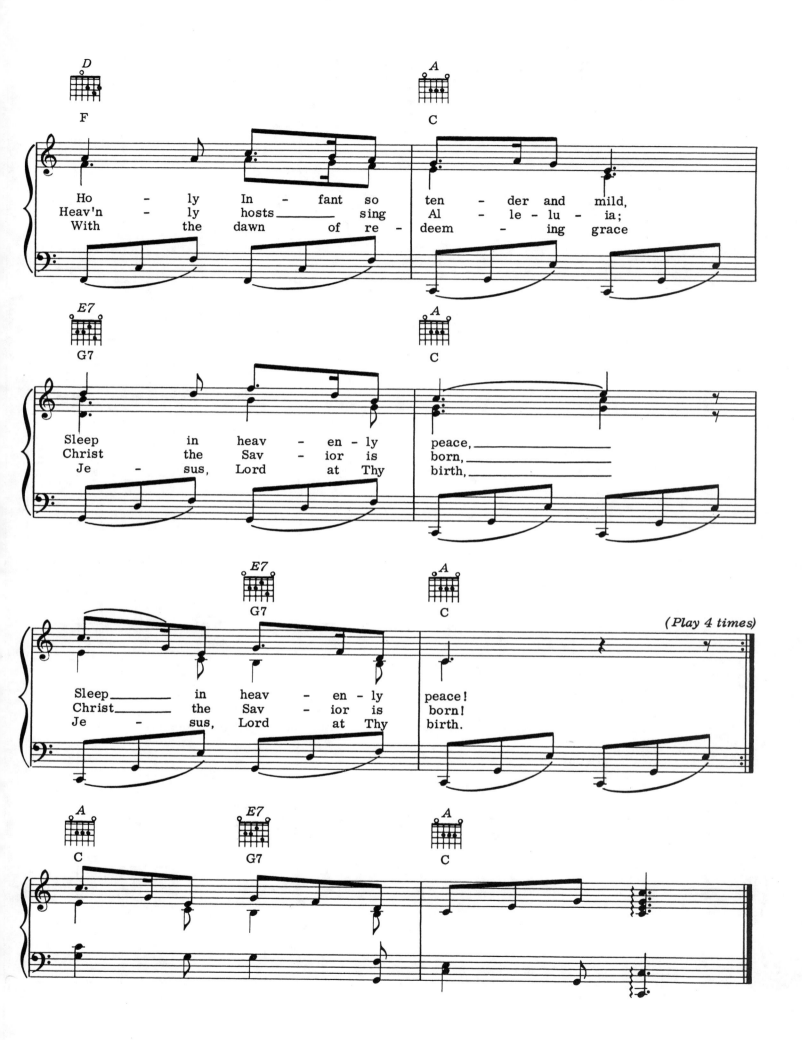

THE TWELVE DAYS OF CHRISTMAS

Traditional English Carol

fifth day of Christ - mas my true love gave to me five gold ____ rings, four ____ call - ing birds, three French hens, two ____ tur - tle doves and a part - ridge ____ in a pear tree. ____ On the

THE VIRGIN MARY

Traditional

WE THREE KINGS OF ORIENT ARE

Words and Music by
John H. Hopkins

Andante

Chorus

Star of won - der, Star of night, Star with roy - al beau - ty bright, West - ward lead - ing, still pro - ceed - ing, Guide us to Thy per - fect light.

Melchior
2. Born a King on Bethlehem's plain,
   Gold I bring to crown Him again.
   King forever, ceasing never,
   Over us all to reign.
   (to Chorus)

Caspar
3. Frankincense to offer have I,
   Incense owns a Deity nigh.
   Pray'r and praising, all men raising,
   Worship Him, God most high.
   (to Chorus)

Balthazar
4. Myrrh is mine, its bitter perfume
   Breathes of life of gathering gloom;
   Sorrowing, sighing, bleeding, dying
   Sealed in the stone-cold tomb.
   (to Chorus)

The Three Kings
5. Glorious now behold Him arise,
   King and God and Sacrifice.
   Alleluia, Alleluia,
   Earth to heav'n replies.
   (to Chorus)

WE WISH YOU A MERRY CHRISTMAS

Traditional English Folksong

With spirit

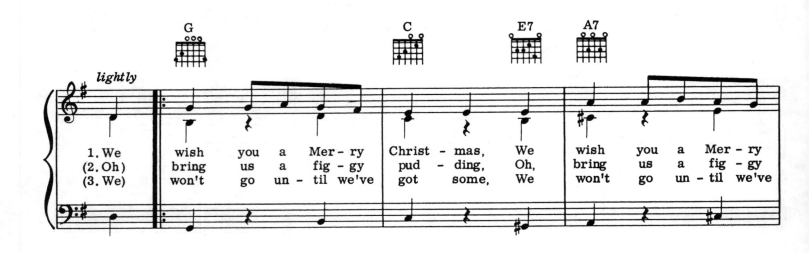

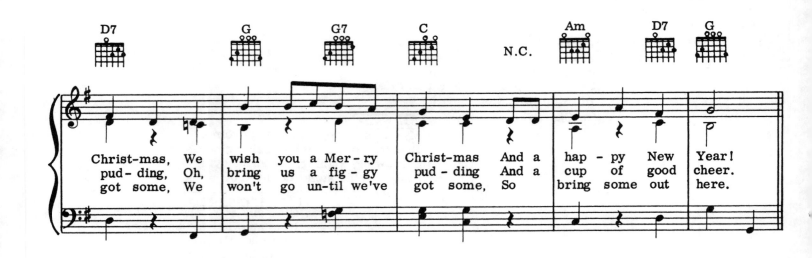

WHAT CHILD IS THIS?

Words by William C. Dix
16th Century English Melody

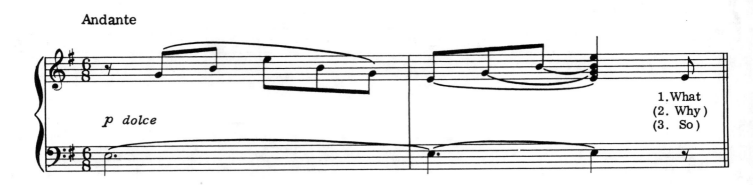

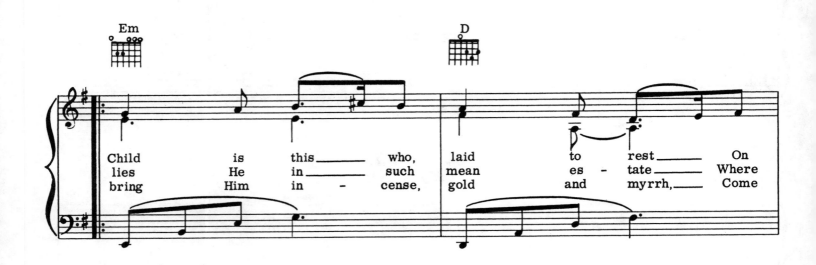

77

D Em B7 Em
an - thems sweet While shep - herds watch are keep - ing?
sin - ners here The si - lent word is plead - ing.
va - tion brings Let lov - ing hearts en - throne Him.
G D Em
This, this is Christ the King Whom shep - herds guard and
B7 G D
an - gels sing: Haste, haste to bring Him laud, The
Em B7
1. 2.
Em
3.
E
Babe, the Son of Ma - ry. 2. Why
3. So
Ma - ry.

SILVER BELLS

Words and Music by Jay Livingston
and Ray Evans

Moderately

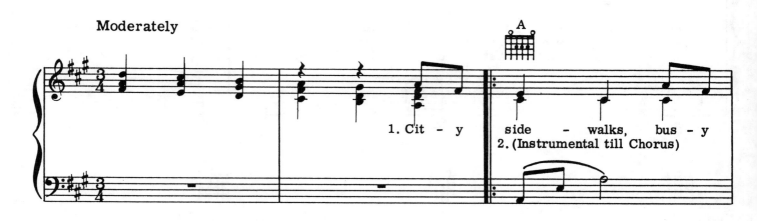

1. Cit - y side - walks, bus - y
2. (Instrumental till Chorus)

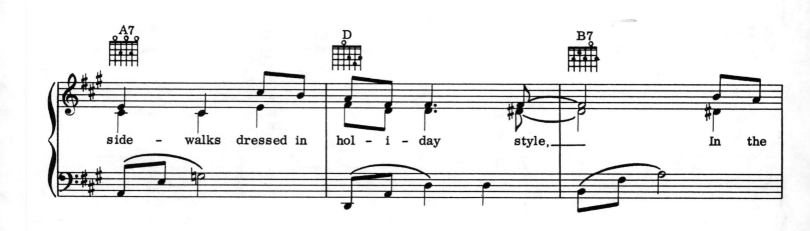

side - walks dressed in hol - i - day style,___ In the

air there's a feel - ing of Christ - mas. Chil - dren

laugh - ing, peo-ple pass - ing, meet-ing smile af - ter smile, And on

ev - 'ry street cor - ner you hear:

(sil-ver bells)   (sil-ver bells)

Sil - ver bells,   Sil - ver bells,

It's Christ - mas time in the cit - y.